Jeremy Toombs

FAIR TO MIDDLIN'

Hog Press, an imprint of
Culicidae Press®
PO Box 5069
Madison, WI 53705-5069
USA
hogpress.com
editor@hogpress.com
+1 (352) 215-7558

HOG PRESS

FAIR TO MIDDLIN'

ISBN: 978-1-68315-170-8

Our books may be purchased in bulk for promotional, educational or
business use. Please contact your local bookseller or the Culicidae Press
Sales Department at +1-352-215-7558 or by email at
sales@culicidaepress.com

culicidaepress.bsky.social – facebook.com/culicidaepress
threads.net/@culicidaepress – instagram.com/culicidaepress
x.com/culicidaepress

Design by polytekton © 2025

Table of Contents

After Charles Olsen
December 12 2020

this moment quiet
          present

the boy starts to moan
                    from a banged ankle

oh, let us adore him
          in his scarecrow base

          where we are
                         everybody is
               who was
the war dead fighting still for
          something
                    for glory
for God for country for king

the crown gets heavier as it loses
influence gets heavier on the whole country

who can we adore when the pandemic
plague adores nothing
like a tornado in a Tennessee trailer park
neighbours disappeared

            tossed over the state line
the twister just bounced
                              over us
the next one won't miss
            or it will
who knows?
            what'll happen next?
                        what's happening now?
no answers
stop asking

the eldest sings out nonsense
                  while jumping down stairs
it's a good an answer as any
good day good night good grief

Last Night: Bats

Benny's first sight
flit before the eyes
thought it was a bird, he did

I said: bat

look around: see 'em all over

Emily Dickinson Derivative

Humid—so close
Escape—Go—
Where could I?
Nowhere.

We are surrounded—grossly—
       intertwined—sublimely—

The only way to get away:
Death—He's timely.

Mood Indigo—Monk

Did you feel free?
How you played them keys
          just like yourself?
here   and   there
                              now
     and   then   yang and
          yin

bass creeps in from out back
that swing comes upriver from New Orleans

What were you thinking about Monk?
(What did Monk thunk?)

All those white folks
watchin' you, listinening—

What can I say now, decades later?
I'll say I don't understand musically...
Don't know how it felt
                    being Monk

Here I am now
taking notice just the same

Five-Fifteen Steak and Eggs

This little boy wouldn't stay in bed
so now it's five-fifteen steak and eggs
listening to Johnny Cash
buttered toast, horse radish
eggs over easy
steak in yolk
wide awake and tired
early morning ain't no joke
but if you must be out of bed
ain't nothin' better than five-fifteen steak and eggs

How Does He Know
--in response to Carl Sandburg's
'Why Do the Children'

how does he know
     which chips to eat,
     which chips to throw?

chip to hand
chip to mouth
chip to floor
     instantaneous decision
eat one, throw one, eat one more
     no deliberation
throw one, throw two, throw three
hold on out to give to me

how does he know?
just because: baby child mind knows

Long Ago

Seen a Shooting Star Tonight
against long time leftover
faraway rain clouds

uncountable stars
    light from long ago ends
    ends in my eyes

tractor lights, neighbor's farm
    clanging and banging
    runnin' about
    lights from the tractor
    in my eyes

remembering them tractors
    runnin' around
    workin' around Tennessee/Kentucky
    tobacco patches
    and goddamn a man
    runnin' a high boy tractor
    so fast
    we're spraying round-up
        god knows what else
    splashed, sprayed, soaked
        shirts, skin, trousers

Strange
        them things
a fallin' star
        shines a light on
long ago

I seen a shooting star tonight
    against long ago past days
 faraway memories
        time as fleeting
      as a shooting star's light

Five Bells
—a conversation

A pub, I said a little louder.

Write it down, he said, not hearing or understanding my accent.

A pub, The Five Bells, a pub, I said.

A pub? There's only one pub: The Five Bells, he said.

Yeah, that's where I need to go!

Should I Do Therapy?

should I talk about it all?
      abuse   neglect   love   longing
      mum   dad's gone   adoption
      trauma   experience   things I've done
       places I've been?
tell it to a stranger?

what if
I cry (sometimes happens)
scream (as I once did)
rock back and forth (done that; mama said, 'Stop it; people might think
something's wrong.')
incriminate myself (no comment)
walk out
run out
run out sweating and screaming

what if I don't like
what the therapist says, doesn't say
how they sit there, thinking about me
how they'd know something about me
how they'd think they know something about me?

shouldn't I just
drink whiskey
practice tai chi and kung fu
write it out   sort myself out
shout it out when nobody's around
cry on my own to Haggard and Jones
repress repress repress
pick on my psychosomatic psoriasis
smoke my mind
drink wine (right now)?

enough of this now.
Therapy, hell.
I feel worse just thinking about it.

Bus Duck

I heard it was a duck
    what a boy snuck
in a bag on a bus
    city kid he was
how odd to snuck a duck

Process

just look:
world's wet
bird on a wind
bird's twittering
not quite a strong breeze
Snow White on for the boys

I suppose it's more than looking
more than listening
mind   heart
          right calm of frazzled
Can you hear
          your own thoughts?
Write them down in voice and verse
          in your own found rhythms

Further to do, just these three things:
          drink 300 cups, Li Bai would say
          read aloud 1,000 poems, I say
          and write and write and write

On Watching Paint Dry, Drinking Alone, Thinking of Little Ol' Me, Listening to Rexroth

listening to Rexroth reading translations
of Chinese poems about drinking
while waiting on paint to dry
and also, I am drinking, thinking.
Rexroth poetry crowd laughing---

Found out more from Mama 'bout them early days of mine adopted into the Toombs clan
                        at eighteen months old:
                                Covering up my ears
                                Wouldn't talk; just screamed.

rearrange
find
long
unknown

Daddy thought: We might've made a mistake. I think he's brain-damaged, mentally retarded, or something along those lines.

find the long unknown
rearrange it
bring it to the fore
why, before you know it you don't know nothing
nothing's really happened.

So long ago I came into this family—it's all I remember—this family that doesn't say 'love' with words, doesn't hug, no touching, really, except for belts, yard sticks, plastic clothes hangers, switches (you had to get your own switch from a tree, not too big, not too small—balance between an acceptable switch and one that wouldn't hurt too much). How could I learn love, how to love? Screaming was natural.

tired, sad fog
drunken   somber.
the effect moves on
like a river calling back
sorrow from the wind.

*No more Bio-Mom (Rhonda), no more Bio-Granny (Carol), no more Bio-Grandad
(Bussy), no more Jeremy (me) in Illinois. Of course, I covered my ears and screamed.
At eighteen months old, the neurological foundation has been laid down; the child's
attachment to its parents/carers will play a large part in determining how the child
forms and maintains relationships in the future. Significant trauma at this time,
such as being separated from the birth parents, such as suffering physical abuse, such
as being really fucking angry, could result in delayed physical, emotional, and mental
development.*
Of course, I covered my ears and screamed.

imaginary world (it's real) in the evergreens in the Chinese mountains so high
there's only clouds night time black trees black mountain black mood in these
mountains alone no sun (my wife and boy out of town and I'm watching paint
dry listening to Rexroth drinking beer) nobody's ever painted these mountains
royal regatta number two or Pugin red they've just always been black never
any sun listening to Chinese poems Rexroth reading 'em brings to mind my
mountain (imaginary real) thinking drinking beer alone all alone watching paint
dry listening to Rexroth

*Questions: Did Rhonda give me away because she loved me? What did Bussy say
about it? Carol? How long did it take for my new parents to love me? After I quit
covering my ears, after screaming? Things I know: My mom screamed, yelled, shouted,
hit, because her dad screamed, yelled, shouted, hit. Constant threat of physical or
emotional abuse leads to heightened levels of cortisol which can cause hyperawareness.*

When the mind is constantly in a high level of alertness, mental abilities such as concentration and short-term memory are compromised.

Who do you love? Tell me: who do you love?
I don't know. I don't know. I don't know. I don't know.

evergreen trees black on the mountainside
clouds in the sky: black
sun is nowhere

should I do therapy?
I should do therapy
sit there on the leather couch saying I felt like covering my ears
felt like screaming
then cover my ears and scream
rock back and forth and scream
I don't know I don't know I don't know

royal regatta number two Pugin red
sitting drinking Cobra
writing random words from Rexroth's space poems
billion years
dark plume
nebula river
Haley's comet
over the Andromeda
[river moon Tao supreme ultimate]
watching the paint dry
listening to Rexroth
drinking beer
thinking

The Big Bang: just a theory, just like
Rhonda's love. Nobody knows
how existence started; I don't know how I started

You got to look back a far piece to know anything at all
about existence, about love.

Was it there, Love? Where did it go, Love?
I don't know. It's just a theory
I was loved.

The mic picks up Rexroth turning pages. Rexroth talking about an aardvark and interrupting his own poem to ask how much time. I'd say: Well, Ken, you got as long as you goddamn please.
After all, he's Ken Rexroth.

and me, now?
I'm sitting here
screaming inside
listening to Rexroth
drinking beer
screaming
watching the paint dry

Helicopter
-after bell hooks

bird call
beech tree
pink apple blossom
bare limbs reflected over the river
rocks seen one foot down
air bubble ripples (from what?)
woodpecker heard
tweet, trill
bark
wood pigeon coo
roar of near weir
flowers on the bank, in the water
duck
helicopter
helicopter
helicopter

Highway 51 Liberation

Part I

This is another highway—Highway 51—coursing through south central Illinois straight as. There's no Highway 51 blues for me, no. My highway blues is out on 41. 51 I'm not tied to it anymore than these four wheels going 70, 35 through town. Through Macon's 1.43 square miles. Around Moweaqua, what little there is. Radford's one remaining official resident. Assumption. Pana. Oconee. Ramsey. Vandalia with the Kaskaskia running through. Sloborier. Vernon. Patoka (pop. 584). Sandoval former sundown town no black allowed round after the sun goes down—These things, these names I don't know. This thread I must've followed in 1979 on my way out. I don't suppose I would've been able to see out the window; for the best I reckon. I've never mourned for forlorn Illinois. Never before thought there's much worse off than Guthrie, Kentucky, highway 41 coming through, coming and going—that's my blues. But for somebody else out there this highway 51 blues is real.

Part II

Indian chiefs and daughters, rich man, poor man, no black man allowed; a thread broken—I picked it up and ran along three, four, five times and felt the pain of leaving, feel the pain now of driving back down, the pain of all those that stayed.

An imagined life I'm driving through looking at all this—I might just have made it to Kentucky all the same. This highway 51 ain't nothing. Nothing to it. Maybe those folks that left and stayed would beg to differ.

Part III

drug dream haze lost alternate past thank goodness thank God for escape not found in needle and nose abuse that can't be papered over with cheeseburgers and toys more persistent real multiple ongoing traumas engulfing whole towns now full of ghosts and empty a haunting pervades the mind and this thread of loss and gloom I've never lived echoes in imagination and some shared memory like little sister said: I'm the lucky one.

Yardstick

I remember many times the yardstick, often with *Elkton Band And Trust* in green, breaking on my be-hind (better keep those hands away). Always rapid fire: whack whack whack whack whack—but quicker than you can say it and sometimes I'd feel it and hear it: *snap*. Break in two.

What was being measured? Reaction time? Pain endurance? The amount of self-control to keep the hands away? I measured out a small dose of joy (hidden) when the yardstick broke; as I got older, as the absurdity became apparent, I'd hold in no small amount of laughter.

> so many years later
> what's a broken yardstick
> but a sign of triumph?

Infinite Patchwork Sphere Rolling

Patchwork quilts are a part of southern culture. My mammaw would've probably never considered herself integral to any type of culture—she did make patchwork quilts, meatloaf, fried chicken, good good gravy—maybe I should get back to the title: that infinite patchwork sphere rolling after me reoccurringly in the night, a slow rolling, immense, not as fast as a slow jog but infinite in its rolling, in its pursuit just there behind me persistent infinite persistent rolling right after me—I'd look back over my left shoulder, not scared of imminent death but of infinite movement, just slower than a slow jog looking back over my left shoulder at the infinite patchwork sphere rolling persistent, infinitely immense not as fast as a slow jog that infinite patchwork sphere rolling immense persistent infinite and there in my dreams just behind me.

A Lament for Modern Poets
-for BJ Wilson

even after all these years apart
more than two decades
I still know who you are
what's familiar to me

we both love words
the sounds they make
try to find all the ways
to put them on paper
sometimes saying them aloud

I mourn for us both
that life gets in the way
walls block us in
city streets turn us around
how can we get out there
to the mountains and rivers?

'A Poem You Might Want to Write', my Son Said

my son said:
      a fox runs across the road
      one short look
      behind the car
      only its tail
          disappeared

from the table
      he hops down
         all fours
      takes a jaunty gallop, looks back

that's how the fox ran, my son said

Pantoum

accidentally at 5:30
I wake up
look for sumitriptan (relief)
decide to start the day

I wake up
looking east I
decide to start the day
with the less strenuous forms

looking east
I notice minute to minute
the less strenuous forms
as body and mind follow

I notice minute to minute
look for relief
as body and mind follow
accidentally at 5:30

After Reading Maxine Chernoff
or
A Poem Completely Unrelated to Maxine Chernoff

later afternoon gloomy front room curtains opened a hand width let in so
little light lamps off overhead off hand width of sky overcast early autumn sky
overcast maybe just a hand width's worth in any event the sun isn't so hot today
and now on its way to setting

Writer's Block

Allen Ginsberg's mind awareness now consciousness three step writing process good for short poems one two three lines notice you're here notice you notice how does it feel? of course not explicitly *don't show me tell me* that's all there is to it ain't no writer's block and again there ain't no writer's block just write

Fair To Middlin'

Grade of cotton. How you doing? Mammaw's answer and not that she'd graded cotton; maybe she did spot cotton fluff clouds in blue Tennessee Kentucky skies dreaming of another life, thinking of a way out of strife, hard being an alcoholic's wife raising five children and feeling what? Fair to middlin' is what she'd say. A grade of cotton, a barometer for the human condition—somewhat good, could be better [good, fair, middling, ordinary, poor.] Fair to middlin' a descending step in quality but better than ordinary—Mammaw certainly not ordinary [neither her chocolate brownies graded good to better.] As I sit here now, if you say to me: how you doing? I might just say: fair to middlin'.

Darkening and Darker

Light dusk blue sky darkening out over St. Michael's Hill, up towards Pigsty Hill; the same light dusk blue sky, darkening here and there. Lights hovering, shimmying, some flickering, some apparently static. They are all waves coming at the eyes from just a very short time ago and not far away.

Closer in bare black late autumn tree branches are right there just being bare black late autumn tree branches standing out against the late autumn dusk blue sky darkening and darker.

> bare black branches
> darkening blue sky darker
> winter night lights

Thursday Morning

Monk piano solo
TV muted
bare feet and smoke rising
from my second morning cigarette

my peaceful contemplative preparation
for teaching day
with no food in the cupboard
suitable for breakfast
but today is pay day
I'll break fast Friday with eggs

Questions and Answers
or
Why not?

I'd ask...

    ....he'd pause

(has he heard me?)

A puff on his wooden tobacco pipe, one hand on the steering wheel of that baby blue 1984 Dodge Ram pickup truck which was not yet mine and not yet dark blue.

He'd answer. He'd answer as true as a puff and a pause for thought would allow.

> just waitin'
> radio off
> just a puff or two
> he'd answer

Then he'd ask me...some math question.

        I'd pause (pretending to do the sums in my head).
He'd start to walk me through the math: rule of 75, what's this divided by that, that multiplied by this, etc.

oh, the struggle
dyscalculia strong
I wish I'd had a pipe

questions and answers
taken and given
all with good intention

And every now and then, in that 1984 Dodge Ram pickup truck, in a quiet moment, him driving, me riding, out of nowhere:

a howl...
aaa-oooooooo werewolves of London!

Why he do that? That howl? That's one question never asked; an answer being unnecessary or maybe just: Why not?

Stop

The sharp triangle corner of the high rise stood stark against Korean Uijeongbu clear blue summer sky and said to mind: Stop. Mind stopped—just briefly. You wouldn't think a mind could listen to the top corner of a building no matter how blue the sky. Anyway, it was a sky so blue and a sharp stark triangle corner up and across the commonly narrow Uijeongbu side street. So how could a body or a mind for that matter not listen when the triangle corner says: Stop. Mind stopped. I kept walking, I did that day, right past the building, kept walking right into town for some forgotten reason. What do I recall strongly, clearly as truth from two decades ago? How blue the sky, how stark and sharp the corner, how silent, how strong, how it spoke: Stop.

Ray Charles' Modern Sounds in Country and Western Music

Something there is about Ray Charles' Modern Sounds in Country and Western Music what makes an early Sunday morning day better, lighter.

Tightening the bolts on the boy's balance bike, him trying out the wrenches (spanners) putting on his lily pads, learning to cycle in the sunshine, Ray Charles' Modern Sounds in Country and Western Music carrying on through the open back kitchen door.

What we're listening to is actually the Complete Country and Western Recordings which I prefer as it's more country in places than Modern Sounds in Country and Western Music which has a lot of Nashville Sound: chorus (too much), lush string arrangements (any string arrangements too much).

The boy just had a banana apple pouch down his gullet, a mess on his hands, and globs of seemingly already chewed banana apple on his legs, with Johnny Cash and Ray Charles singing *I just don't know when to quit.*

Unyielding Bastards

usury is sin
Nationwide
break down a person's pride
unyielding bastards
tell me about the interest rate
I gotta pay when I take
twenty-five pounds out the ATM
take to the tellers
money sellers
unrepentant bastards

I take cash out
on my card
to take into the bank
and handover to pay
the minimum on my credit card
and she tells me about interest
in that pseudo friendly auto-vox
in a big box of money

I find it funny
y'all sure make a lot of money, I say
you'd be surprised, she says
how much a financial transaction costs

Look Up at the Stars

past midnight
bathroom break
cold
I hear a rustle:
a creature's cautionary hustle
behind my tent, I step out
shine the light about
then I look up at the stars:
       no need to be the learned astronomer
       just gaze in open mouthed open wonder
the Milky way spans across:
       Big Dipper, search for Orion, Taurus
I look down to see badgers rooting about
       in the lower field.
then I look back up...a thought fleeting...seeing back into time

this moment is fine, mine
another brief moment of awareness
as I look back up

English Winter Hangnail Moon Waxing

cool wet December night
soon we will know longer days
ever increasing light
births and deaths
turning and turning
waking up little by little
becoming full
like the English winter hangnail moon waxing

Snow Haiku

snow falls off
branch springs free
three green leaves

Visceral
-from a dream

animal visceral red and red
Taurus bull charging   wrecking
no china shop safe
communists even riding on bulls' backs sanctioned by the state
mechanical bulls paid for by city council
it doesn't stop

women weep   survivors argue
fate doesn't answer
doesn't even hear the howls
fierce animal life skin torn off
and all things dependent upon all things said
as speaking lets out the insides (that and pissing)
and the prison of self is no help
just showing off barnyard blues of howling barking hounds
and a red red rooster strutting through
have you seen him?
fuckin' all the hens
never getting their names
and so worn out that he couldn't even cock-a-doodle doo

Jude the Obscure

there comes a time when springs to mind
all those things that fail

a dark night—star light hidden by clouds
and a shroud over a dream

there's a man walking, bursting his seams
but there is nothing you can see coming out

there is life lived too long, too hard,
no card dealt for benefit

out of all these times
these things
this night
this man
this life
this is illusion of strife
a shifted perspective
the knife comes into the hand
but if you can see the land your feet tread
then there is no drowning

he is walking away
the moon waxed half-way
tomorrow is today
all we have is what we say to ourselves

Medicine, Man (What I Need)

should have known
drowsy
congested
weary
sleepy eyed
should have known
   that medicine, man
   what I need
my own medicine man I am
whiskey in hand
sharp
brings me back round, my medicine, man

On Looking at a Statue of Abraham Lincoln in Parliament Square

what's Abe doing here?
Abraham, oh, Abraham
in London.

what are you doing here?
far, far from that ol' Kentucky home
standing alone looking at Parliament, Big Ben,
hearing those bells toll

What are you doing here?
you could ask me the same thing
being from the same place, now here together
in this same time

Kentucky boys and Illinois too
looking over at Ghandi-Ji, at the back of his head.

What are we doing here, any of us?
Me, Abe Lincoln, Ghandi-Ji?

Truth is: truth is in the air we're breathing.
London, India, Kentucky
Now, 1930, 1865

we all breathe the same
the bells ring through
what we can do, we do
freedom is in everybody's veins

Sam San Shan

three peaks sit
under snow
sunshine's cold
ten thousand things sit

where would I go?
where I've been, where I'm going
is there in the air
where three peaks sit
sam san shan

On Seeing a Friend Early One Morning in an Unusual Place

I saw Mark Anthony Pearce there:
        Cabot Circus traffic pedestrian island
waiting for the light

early morning
walkin' in, men talkin'
talkin' men serious in the early morn
        unshorn
   with great beards

there are times we want to be this way: serious

River Avon Swollen

River Avon swollen
tide's up and high
rain's fallin' in
New Cut Avon runnin' backwards
backwards and full
chocolate milk brown
bank to bank

On Watching Mark Read Poetry

sick, my man Mark
hunched
all shoulder bones
all jaw and brow
skin and bone

all true journeys we take alone
dark ill rant and rail
preach and pray   breath by breath

Wind Blow

wind blow
rain on window
in a bit:
wet bike trip

Red Faced

red faced
Chris hums up high
sings strong
some contraption on the E string, asking:
bring that soul through/funky and high

Words

kafaffle
falafel
palaver

kafalafel
palafel
falaver

problem problem problem

Joshua's Joke

knock knock

who's there?

walks away with a paper cup
on his head

First Day of School
-September 12, 2018

end of Benny's first day
what'd he say?
>   *I'm going to boil you in a stew!*
he said.
he screamed at the deputy head
he said *I'm going to boil you in a stew!*
to the head
the first day
what a way to go!

my little contrary boy
>   felt no joy
at close of day

fight the system! fight the man!
Watch dem close if you can!
boil 'em in stew!
dont't let 'em say
what you should do!

so articulate
so precise
not at all nice
Benny knows what to say—Listen:
>   when they tell you what to do
>   be like Benny
>   what Benny would do:
>   just scream: *I'm going to boil you in a stew!*

Worked up, Trouble

Some folks get worked up. Some folks rebellious by nature, by nurture—just naturally kicking back against the goads. Sometimes you can see it coming, feel it coming if it's you. Creeping in— worked up, obstinate, stubborn, hardheaded, ornery—call it what you will: It has a mind of its own, takes over a mind over whatever matters.

> whatever matters
> about the grey sky daytime
> watch out: there's trouble

I Let a Song Go Out of my Heart

starts out happy
         up-tempo
stays there

save for that middle
         tension, tautness
a conversation 'tween bass and keys

what you sayin' there Monk?
how you hearin' Duke?

I suppose if it was a feeling
you could put into words
you wouldn't be playin' like you do

Poetry Club

the students
are so strange
deranged
shaking their pens
instead of writing
sitting under the table
they have cat ears and laugh uncontrollably

being their teacher: what can I do
but write this down?

Monk, Coltrane, and Little Sleeping Super Sam

little sleeping Super Sam
my a.m. listening
            Monk and Trane laying it down
little sleeping Super Sam laying down

my time shorn by a shakey morning
            from a long, long, last night

now it's easy:
            Monk, Coltrane, and little sleeping Super Sam
            scratching his head
            on a blue sofa bed
            blue blanket warm
            breath in its own time
            Coltrane breathes through that saxophone
            Monk brings lone notes home

the robot clock's eyes
tick tock side to side
the time's right for
Monk, Coltrane, and little sleeping Super Sam

Doc and Bill

sublime sound: high voice and Kentucky mandolin
      that bottom end Deep Gap guitar sound
blended
risin'
takin' us all up with 'em

Street Light Birch Tree Rainy Night Shine

December cold rain
       all day long
come nighttime
all that's seen out the window:

street light birch tree rainy night shine

what's heard?
       rain patter
       wind
       cars coming, going
my wife callin' up for dinner

That Time
or
Competitive by Nature

Oh, that time topping tobacco—that's when the flowers're taken off, topped, to let the bottom leaves fill out. Well, that time on David Glover's we were topping some long ol' Tennessee/Kentucky border burley tobacco double rows; seems they started in Tennessee, ended up in Kentucky. Long rows make a long day. Now, I should say: I'm competitive by nature. So, when I heard this one fella say: *I'm fixin' to pass this son of a bitch* I didn't look over aside from out the corner of my eye. He was three to four double rows over, ten feet back or so. I didn't hesitate more than the quickness of that side eye—just according to my nature I was off & gone, down that double row, flower tops and suckers too off and off down to a foot or so—each hand feeling what to do , moving down the stalk, eyes looking to the next plant—fast, efficient, effortless.

> off & gone
> toppin' out a double row
> down and half back
> not even stopping for water

Ain't That Something

a certain shade sunrise pink red
        coming up onto the clouds
that Townes honky tonk piano
        singing Hank with e-lectric guitar

ain't that something
        morning sunshine backyard
bare shoulders   a bit of time

Two big bright red strawberries
        right in reach
hanging heavy

Ray Charles comin' in
ain't that something

Cat's Paw Prints In the Snow
with Duane Vorhees

flowers in the snow
some ask: where do they go?
like us, to oblivion they go
with the weather change

in the beginning existence was absence
in the end: still nothing
but is there something in the between?

This River Wye Bridge Writes a Poem Itself

the bridge shakes a bit—
cars two meters behind us

long green weeds flow down stream
willows on an island
a dove floats across the sky

the world is full of curious moments
something distinctive
like five poets on a bridge

the poem writes itself

Said Eliot About *The Wasteland*

*-to me it was only the relief of a personal
and wholly insignificant grouse against life;
it is just a piece of rhythmical grumbling.*

that's what it is
       it is
that rhythm that's his
through and through
the downfall of modern times
the blues comes out
through Eliot's lines

last call last call
hurry up please it's time
the fella says

Who's in the pub
       the last hours of the past days

hurry up please it's time
last call last call
       one bourbon   one scotch   one beer
that'll do   that'll do
and Eliot: just another man with the blues

Heard

heard them first
      I did
oh, out of the gloomy soaked
   lowered down night sky
unmistakable honk honk

looked up
      my head torch
catching two geese low
      all dark black under grey
gliding through the temporary light
through and gone

I heard them again
I heard two geese again
      quickly vanish from the sky

Lovely Chat

with my mother-in-law

we discuss Elvis, Dylan, Willie, early and ongoing childhood traumas, how they are still with us

we talk about food   microwaves   warm milk

and all the while she's nibbling like a squirrel the rind of parmesan or getting her steps in or plunging the soapy cafetiere over and over again

always something rhythmic and returning
          in the music   the trauma
how it makes us   stays with us

everything is unusual in life
so very hard to forget

[poetry]

    may make us from time to time a little more aware of the deeper, unnamed feelings which form the substratum of our being, to which we rarely penetrate; for our lives are mostly a constant evasion of ourselves, and an evasion of the visible and sensible world.
    -TS Eliot from The Use of Poetry and the Use of Criticism

evade, evade the poet cries.
it's all non-sense he lies
something deep down, already gone:
leave it! leave it all alone

Pink Goanas

sure are something
        pink goanas
but rare, so rare

the only things known
        about pink goanas
is that they're pink, goanas are
and there's more than one
        pink goanna
could be only two pink goanas—who knows?

could be pink goanas are everything
could be everything pink goanas

Nervous

she's nervous up there
hands shaking
reading poetry too fast
not enough enunciation
nervous she is

the poetry's rhythmic, strong
strong in voice
        from someplace strong and true
there's something she's giving us of herself up there

even as she loses her nerve
        she knows what's important
runs to the back of the room
        has a swallow of beer   comes back up
bashes out her last poem—honest—real
the room applauds
but she's not done—

Out the Window
-after Larry Eiger

long tree February shadows
long halfway across the field
pigeon flies across, goes into the tree line

evergreen, mangnolia
south side shining
slight southerly wind moves
clouds ever so slow

Looking Across the River

creek sound coming in
riverside rushes green on the water
trees rising up yon hill bear no leaves
yet a green tint throughout
against blue sky
                  white clouds   cold northerly

wind ripples water
woodpecker
morning birds
some folks   talking
something silent on a log half-submerged

Benny's Blues

could be anything
what sets the mood
getting down on life (all them rules)
moody morning
don't know what to do
anything can happen
when my Benny's got the blues

won't take no consolation
ain't nothing I can do
just a dire situation
when my Benny's got the blues

could be a sunny day
or clouds hanging low
some simple phrase one might say
that sets him in a mood
can't figure out nothin'
best just let him be
when my Benny's got the blues

On a Date with My Wife Seeing Hokusai and Hiroshige

imagining these woodblock prints
in our living room, bedroom
down the hall walls

imaging ourselves
        in the pictures

'The Amida Falls in the Far Reaches of the Kisukaido Road'

I want to be there in that place
talking about swords, waterfalls
        or more likely
just being there
feeling the mist
and cooking tea

'The Hollow of the Deep Sea Wave off Kanagawa'

what we call 'The Wave'
glad I'm not in those boats
in that water

the wave arching up
steeper than Fuji-San

I'd rather be on the mountain
        even as it exploded

Happy

out and about
early spring wet Sunday

my boys on a bench
          mix of mud, rain, ice cream
on clothes, face, hands

happy

Sam's Shadow Tai Chi

Sam's shadow
      swims with the clouds
Sam himself?
      he's the sun

Dissolution of the Abbey

Is that what happened here?
glory's gone by
bricked up doors
ain't nothing made to last

Out the Window

government guidelines childminding
statutory reforms pedagogies
zoom online meeting powerpoint presentation

dark clouds massed
slowly moving east
out the window
moving through to inside
bird song coming through

Just Wondering

what my own birth was like?
I was there of course.
I don't remember a thing of course.

was I foot first like my own second born?
      come out kicking
      come out blue, floppy
was it a normal birth?
      head first? come into this upside down
      maybe the cord around my neck
      turning me a bit blue like my first born?

if I were to go in for hypnosis
what would I find
going back forty-three years and then some
to the day my face saw the world?
      hospital? bedside?
      Mother's smile?
      her fear—no father around?

anyway, what's it matter?
forty-three years and then some later
could've been born an alligator

doesn't matter
I was just wondering

My Response to *The Well-Wrought Urn*
from *The Art of Writing*

old masters? ha.
they haven't seen
out my morning window so how could
they write *blue gray cloud pink sky out the window looking east*

a moment in ink can't be erased
who cares if I satisfy myself or not?

Winter England

Lordy, lordy I ain't hardly
stopped all the day long.
Should be happening shortly,
but then I could be wrong.

Gray skies, clouds, and rain
falling out of the sky.
Got a left-leg pain—
don't really know why.

Wind is blowin' tree tops around;
all things covered in gloom.
Once the light all dies down
winter England's a goddamn tomb.

Piece by Piece

arms just so
straight
      near to perpendicular
things placed just so
      arms   legs   words
step behind   around
      just there in video
          on the page
pattern   now the mind
      the body
foot   hand   heart   fingers
        joints small and large
a jump
something not yet done   over and over
    piece by piece
perfection comes when the words
          the moves
      feints   and steps
          are more imbedded
in body   in mind
    over time
piece by piece

Eight and Six

speaking out, out of mind something
to turn to another time
of a life given over to love

marking time aloud
every known thing shaking
all unknowns speculated on
and on till sleep comes on

it ain't nothing that I still do
praying praying praying
what I know is nothing ever happened
what can I expect now?

so closely finely wrought
bones heart sinew neurons
presenting as anger mostly
but in truth? all is pain

it's all pain   too much pain

Land Between the Lakes Suite

all them times
all them times
          I drift away
spread sheets   functions
ninety percent of this
          half of that
all them times   like now
          drifting away
                    eyes following
a wind-borne osprey over Energy Lake shoreline

osprey's circling
another just rose up out the water
          ten inch trout clawed
flying off

carp thrashing in the shallow reeds and flooded trees
          struggling
what are they doing in there?

life's hard
is something to learn
tooth and claw thrashing muscles
ain't none of us getting out

          *

between the rivers canal
one hundred yards across or so

speedboat wake slaps the shore
outboard sound fading out

an overcast day
not a sunny side in sight
how can we keep to something that is unseen?

hold the thought in mind
we can only bide the time
always something down the line
these days   these days   these days
no thing turning out fine

         *

the sign for the boat ramp, sticking up out of high water
must've been a half hour, an untold number of rocks
picked out, dug up, hurled, heaved, skipped, thrown shotgun style
got close   not close   everyone of them rocks hit the water
not one goddamn rock hit that goddamn sign

Frog Mill Suite and Buddhafield Poems

Frog Mill Suite

sunset, moonrise
    on a purple moor
sheep off to the south
masses of clouds float by
    on northwest wind

at the top of Frog Mill: eight-hundred-year-old mill ruins
        Devapriya's stupa looking over it all

     *

waxing moon
        near to half full
up half way
        in a light blue sky
what are we doing here?
just waiting around, looking at the clouds

     *

two blue jet aeroplanes
        southeast to northwest
          and vice versa
low low low   just above the moor
so so so fast sound lags behind
two blue jet aeroplanes
        slipping so low, so fast
across the vast blue blue sky

     *

a shooting star   a fox
clear night sky   light of the waning moon

up late talking: spiritual matters
mind matters

                    *

Friday night Throwleigh church bells
ring out from up the hill
half an hour's walk away

the sound carries down the valley's
down to this Frog Mill   full of joy
full of the sound of these church bells

Jesus, Buddha: realized beings still speaking
sounding out for centuries   millennia old now
talking about sangha   fellowship

now look how we go through this old world
not listening,
save for when somebody else   from somewhere,
comes along and says this: shut up and listen

                    *

moon peaks up
            over cloud cover
midges flying around my face
I'm on baby sleep duty
wishing for a cup of tea

off in the distance
I hear a girl yell:
            I am a whirlwind!

moon now comes out waxing gibbous
          disappears back into the clouds

                    *

top field Frog Mill
seeing into the valley
hearing joy below
Dartmoor rising up off behind me

a grey gathering of clouds
slow moving under the blue yonder
wind rustling trees,
voices in the hedge—illicit?
                              Who knows?
I know
there is peace
blowin' around here
                    somewhere
in my mind

          *

sunset clouds over my shoulder
last bright pink sunset clouds

          *

morning mist
blown gentle on a southerly
floating

white ball sun
          unhot
mist covered

Lotus flip flopping
          across the field

Bex and the boys
            early Frog Mill storytime
just sitting here writing lines

                *

eastern sky clouds
painted on blue
imperceptible north-east drift

subtle dusk
voices across fields
children

cut grass   dry   hard
felt like a piece went right in my foot

                *

stay for a week
lasts for a year
change of heart
comes round here
Frog Mill: time is still
changes the mind
strengthens the will
back again and back again
no other friend
like Frog Mill

                *

Legendary: Froggy Mill Froggy Mill Froggy Mill (the song goes); a giant frog out
of the mill, shocking
            stars, rain showers—there are powers here not seen on any other
scene—powers here in mind, powers here untold in real time at Frog Mill.
That little boy of mine running around not needing his daddy, his mummy;
memories of me, a grown man, needing my daddy, my mommy, needed to
do something I'd not thought of before; late night deep thoughts, deep talks,

reading into old memories locked away: my brother, other brothers, my mother, my bio-mother, haven't really considered my other daddy (he absconded, left, flew the coop, chickened out) and my daddy I know always gone, and thinking just yesterday I'd not go down any dark holes this time around, but here we are making memories by remembering a time when reaction was unconsidered, but here at Froggy Mill, shit does get real. How do I feel around strangers? How do I feel faceblind, unable to recognize folks I've known for years now? And then a presence met on the land in form of a fox, a river dragon, those shooting stars, talking and talking about faeries, about mind mind mind mind mind mind. You know, here at Froggy Mill, you don't know where you might go. Who's in control? Who knows? Anything can happen.

On Show
-Things Said

joy
imagination
it bears reiteration
tradition   creation
          tension
intention is from the heart

and another thing:
                    a deep sense of trust
[everything everywhere all at once]
                              in a flow
not a conscious thing, imagination
could never imagine
          such things as I've imagined
doesn't have to be as it's always been
nothing ever has been as it's always been

in an ideal world
spin the wheel
spin the wheel
where it lands
is what is real

what is happening?
   is it now?
who can do it?
   gotta know how

birth and death
and all in between
let me look at the the map....
where we're going
depends on where we've been

five minutes left
till the end of time
voices long unheard
coming down the line

let's bring it together somehow
how? how? does anybody know?
work it out and work it out
keep it centered on the heart
the results
         are on show

August 6th, 2022
Saturday
Frog Mill
Buddhafield Village Retreat

pink cirrus clouds
sunset down beyond the moor
tender blue sky goes so well
        with pink cirrus clouds
    wispy   scattered somewhat
        over the tender blue sky

I call Benny over to look
    look at that, I say
I think those are cirrus clouds
        and that blue
        my favourite sky
as I'm looking up, the boys says nothing
        drifts off towards camp

now he's wanting to fight
        double back fist
looping left and right
toward the chest   we play
I practice grabbing punches
        it ain't easy
                grabbing punches
the boy wins

the boy puts on pyjamas
asks for milk
chat with Jo
asks to sit at the fire
talks to Theo
half a dozen askings and actions
        just to get to ten o'clock bedtime

I don't mind so much
my boy
time with my boy:
better than pink cirrus clouds
tender blue sky
sun setting beyond the moor

Naga Ritual
-w/ my boy the elder

mantra: Om namo bhagavatayai arya prajnaparamitayai

right next to the band we sit
powerful
vibes from the guitar
        from the drum
shruti box   horns   flute   bass   drum drum drum

my boys voice and mine: Om namo bhagavatayai arya prajnaparamitayai
breathing in one hundred and eight times and then some
        some more for good measure

so wide open
tears streamin'
holidin' my boy on my lap
him on the hand cymbals
on and on and on again
wide open free
 it's all love really all it is ain't nothing more to say:

    Om Bhagavan namo bhagavatayai arya prajnaparamitayai

Surprise Buddhafield Day

watching my boy from the kula, working out how he's feeling from how he's feeling, walking, sitting...I can see that he needs something—something always some thing he's had trouble asking for—I sit there watching, lost in his thoughts, opened up to feelings, opened up the heart: get it out, get it out. What can I do? Ain't no fixin' some things—some things just things is what they are.

burnt arm
busted elbow
my kid's struggles
naga ritual

These are a few of some powerful things in a surprise Buddhafield day—something in the way, and something opened up—heart, I suppose—tell me, who knows what I am supposed to do now?

Buddhafield Blues

them cows lowing
knowing the blues
bellowing it all out to the night

so many stars out
can't hear nothing
just sitting there
light from the past present to the eye

somebody walkin' by   dishes rattlin'
a car down the road
darker outline of tree line against the sky
dog barking after midnight
        that ain't no good sign to a superstitious body

 a moment of silence
        where I'm just listening
a moment of joy there
        where I'm just crying
a moment of fear there
        I didn't know what to do
a moment of compassion there
        I got some help
and again and again
        a word   a hug   a hand
there are all these moments: I'm open

What am I supposed to do now?

Men's Poetry Workshop

poetry and more poetry
reading and writing are good
it's the sharing that's valuable

the air a bit still
heated
try to stay in the shade and still

books all over the floor
all of them speaking
speaking—speaking of all the things

there's a party happening
it's not here
here is very serious
            these men all these words

Compost Loo

sitting in the compost loo
a knock on the door
at least I'm not alone

August 10th, 2022 Frog Mill

The big dipper—part of the big bear Ursa Major—slowly falling down toward 2am, just level and the bottom flat against the solid black mass of tree line silhouetted in the brightness of a just not full moon rising up from the opposite side of Frog Mill—Blackaton Brook winding its way between the two from a certain perspective.

Aeroplane engines push across the sky just in front of the noise to the north, voices across the field: a riotous laughter, dogs barking, sheep bleating, cows lowing, footsteps darkly walking by brushing the grass—Wren coughs in the nearby tent—a zip opens—more footsteps—youngsters voices, young folks wanting Pringles, thinking of themselves from a certain perspective

Inside ourselves there's awareness, a width and breadth, a filling up and an emptying out—pouring out and healing up—some serious things change, turn, become untrue and how we laugh and cry both at the healing and the pain— who can ever know just what might happen? Could be anything to change your perspective.

These Buddhafield Kids

oh they can be wild
       these Buddhafield kids
running around
dysregulated
punching bread
imagining stools are bumper cars

but right now   during meditation,
       these Buddhfield kids
are quietly engaged
independent
drawing and colouring
             all over their faces

These Buddhafield Adults

oh these Buddhafield adults
         look at them
sitting there
eyes closed meditating
at least pretending to meditate

imagining   imagining   imagining

         that these Buddhafield kids
who've stopped colouring their faces and turned up their collective volume

         these Buddhafield adults imagining that these Buddhafield kids
                  aren't even there

She Holds the Center True

ah there she is
        right at the center
holding the room
radiating outwards
        warmth and light
the day and the night

how it'd all fall apart
haw it'd all fall down
how it's all from the heart
how now here we are
        so many moons later
a smaller circle sure
        a circle so sure pure perfect
like a Dolly Parton song and like Emmylou
like the sun shining through

the rest of us know what to do
keep moving around and around
as she holds the center true

Look at Him there

Bohdi Bohdi
true to his name
wouldn't be the same
without that face that smile
        in a Buddhafield space
just like Buddha

but today
        today that Bodhi
he wiped his face
        with a cheeky grin
he wiped his face
        on my shirt

So True

lo...hark yon sounds
      a fiddle low and sweet
my child's laugh
      his friends talking
a girls' chorus
a younger child's squeal
a few birds
      still the bow moves
          to the false finish
starts off again jauntily
      flowing up into the blue sky
                  across the field
moved by the breeze   moved this heart
      a fiddle low and sweet
What else is there so true?

BOB Morning Breakfast
AKA Space Girl Pukes
AKA Thinking of Padmapani

crumpets, toast, tea
all on the fire in the tepee
Flo reading Space Girl Pukes

The kids also:
    writing drawing thinking
about Padmapani—all his life
dedicated   concentrated,
        tuned into a life
                lived in full
so full:
        full of mischief love Nagas
pujas laughter....surely all of the feelings
        and so many of the ten thousand things
                have passed through the mind and heart

and here we are now at BOB morning breakfast
        thinking of Padmapani
        eating crumpets and toast
        listening to Space Girl Pukes

Raising a Tipi to Scale

one inch to a foot
a bed sheet cut
a pack of skewers
half-hitches with canvas thread
       Annie somehow had in her pocket
      with a pen knife   tipi diagrams
      and lord knows what else

a dozen or so of us
       stuck in
making scale tipis
imagining douglas fir poles in hand
the lift of the tripod
the rope in hand
lashing the canvas down

imagining the heft of the canvas
      the unfurling—all this done to scale
      and to be done in full

knowledge given
knowledge known
the doing done together
      coming together
so many things to come to one

Two Days In

leg sore-left thigh
right foot's better

the second field is filling up
        friends   strangers
some known as friends
some known as strangers
        knowns
        known unknowns
        unknown unknowns

things run together year to year
        camp to camp
it's all one song
        one continuous river
            people time
        the water itself: through the woods
                under the bridge
           barely over the rocks
              then deepening
          then who knows what happens
          as the water goes
as the water goes round the bend?

voices afar
high and low
laughing
clear unclear

the high tree line silhouette
up against the darkening blue sky

      *

ah the beginning
        the four directions
        wild oats sown
70's jazz fusion horns blown

a circle complete
a retreat from distractions
        into wind into fire into earth into water

smoke in the air
rain in the air falling on the earth

for what it's worth
in this at the start,
 something has moved: mind and heart

                    *   *   *

Lotus, Ruth, Bex
        there in a huddle
        holding the middle
        like playing a fiddle

                    *   *   *

it's the people, innit?

Padmapani blowing that horn
Rebecca's laugh carrying across the field
Annie across the circle, hands together
Three children huddled together
Three folks sat around the fire Buddha
        chanting, smiling

rain falling soft and fine
                    nobody minds
        something we can find
              in all the people
                         the people
        it's the people, innit?

*

morning view through the tent flaps

slant of sunlight enters

slight wind shakes the grass
              moves the morning dew
everything sparkles and shines
              dances around

I've slept such a long time
              11.00 – 8.00
such long dreams
              two long dreams
                         staying with me

a violent basketball game
              punches and three point shots

another life of mine
              a different persona
                         an intense platonic affair played out
finishing at Pickford House? (I might have dreamed here before—hard to tell)

So many unusual things
              sleep, lucid dreams
dew dancing in sunlit grass
              what's it all mean?

Beyond Actions

how can we navigate all of this?
all this turmoil   joy   silence   noise?
by the moonlight perhaps?
just keep watch

       but moonlight can't be trusted
       just reflection
             mutable
       like this human condition
             sad and happy

just saying please and thank you
please somehow hold me
thank you for seeing me
please be kind when you can
thank you for seeing beyond actions

Fathers

I

so many fathers
            gone
        not even fathers one could say
no way knowin'
        how things might've been
if things had been another way

II

in a tent
in a field
edge of Dartmoor
middle of rain and wind blowing
my boy sleepin'
and I'm right here

III

it's a whole side of a child
            unknown
    with the father gone
nothing known of blood and bone
                what made us boys
        of fathers gone

IV

there goes my friend
                a man
child held in hand
        held in heart
some fathers
        always there
at least we're tryin' to be

V

compassion's hard
      on another level
maybe there was
          no kind of choice
runnin' away
sayin' 'not mine'
who cares? what's to blame?
they've done been gone
      just the same

VI

hearts open
          raw   vulnerable
    held
  safe
these men and the kids
we ain't going nowhere

VII

that's one good thing
      stickin' around
solid
      feet and heart grounded
something's right
something's wrong
but it's side by side
      all this life long

www.ingramcontent.com/pod-product-compliance
Lightning Source LLC
Chambersburg PA
CBHW081146020426
42333CB00021B/2685